Lucid Dreaming

Essential Information On Enhancing Sleep Quality And Cultivating Creativity Through The Regulation Of Dream States

(Embarking On A Quest For Spiritual Liberation Through The Exploration Of Consciousness)

Charles Laurence

TABLE OF CONTENT

Basic Concepts

A "Lucid Dream" may refer to a dream that occurs during the REM stage of sleep, at which point the dreamer becomes consciously aware that they are dreaming, and consequently remains in this state without awakening. The distinctive state of consciousness is referred to as "clarity" or "being clear-headed."

In addition to the attribute of clarity, distinctions between Lucid and conventional dreams will encompass the following (this enumeration may not be exhaustive):

The subsequent dream is significantly more indelible than a non-lucid dream.

It appears to be further pronounced;

The individual harbors the firm belief that he or she assumes an active role as an engaged participant in the dream, as opposed to assuming a passive role as a mere observer;

The individual with aspirations is prepared to engage in actions autonomously;

The individual who envisions is prepared to exert influence over the backdrop and substance of the vision through a deliberate act of focus.

The visionary is also empowered to influence the manner in which they engage with the dream - for instance, engaging in actions that would not typically be possible in waking life, such as altering their bodily form, traversing solid objects, levitating, soaring through space, teleporting to remote locations, traversing through time, and so forth.

The primary factors that may lead to the disappointment of individuals' expectations regarding any lucid dream encompass:

Insufficient proficiency in the practice of Lucid dreaming; Inadequate knowledge and skills pertaining to Lucid dreaming; Limited expertise in the domain of Lucid dreaming;

Lack of practice;

Noncompliance with one or more fundamental rules or principles;

There exists a particular element within your subconscious that exerts influence over the subject matter of your dreams.

The resolution to the primary can be readily achieved by diligently implementing the principle of practice leading to proficiency. A novice may observe an enhancement in the caliber of their dreams within a matter of days, however, lucid dreaming is not an instantaneous occurrence, but rather a skill that must be cultivated gradually. I have indeed encountered a comprehensive guide that claims it is possible to acquire a highly proficient level in an associate degree program within a span of just one month. However, this assertion is not particularly beneficial, as it is considered insufficient for many individuals due to its brevity. Hello, as you consistently engage, you need only concern yourself with the fact that you are making gradual progression, albeit in small increments.

The solution to the second will be same merely, however may be tougher to attain in reality: "shore up your resolve". The exclusive method to sustain the perpetuity of practicing Lucid Dreaming. While you may lack a specific rationale for clear dreaming, it is nonetheless advisable to engage in such practice to maintain one's proficiency. If, for any reason, you fail to dream with clarity on a particular occasion, it is imperative that you adhere to the prescribed method to the best of your ability. By doing so, you will enhance the prospects of achieving success on a subsequent occasion. Conversely, failing to practice this approach diminishes the likelihood of favorable outcomes. If you prolong your absence without applying for a considerable duration, you will inevitably be required to accept the consequences and recommence your endeavor as if you were an absolute novice. Lucid dreaming is an immensely valuable skill to acquire, and should you decide to pursue it, you must be prepared to exert significant effort, just as you would for any endeavor of great worth.

The resolution for the third issue lies in approaching lucid dreaming in a manner akin to conducting a scientific experiment: systematically identify any errors or oversights, take note of them, and subsequently undertake a revised attempt to rectify those missteps. The Dream Diary holds significance in this context, which I will elaborate on later. It proves valuable because it enables you to evaluate your performance objectively.

The resolution to the fourth issue is further nuanced, generally the underlying problem becomes explicitly evident within the dream itself, yet on other occasions it remains covert. Typically, it is something relatively inconsequential; in general, it is a prolonged accumulation of repressed recollection. I urge the reader to acquaint themselves with established literature on the subjects of science and psychology. In the field of Alchemy, it is observed that the prima material possesses a state of putrefaction prior to any attempt being made to transmute it into a valuable substance. Likewise, the conscious awareness of one's repressed emotions can induce a decay of the spiritual essence. It is never pleasant to discover that you have been harboring a sentiment that goes against your own rationality. It is thus highly unpleasant that initially you may be inclined to doubt the information when it is presented to you. Nonetheless, due to their significant impact on the subconscious mind, it is inevitable that repressions will also exert an influence on the quality of your lucid dreaming experience. In order to attain mastery over lucid dreaming, it is imperative to also gain mastery over one's unconscious mind…

The Advantages of Engaging in Lucid Dreaming

In addition to the enjoyment derived from immersing oneself in the realm of a lucid dream, there exist numerous additional advantages of significant magnitude. The profound sense of assurance that arises from the encounter with a realm devoid of any apprehensions or restraints is truly remarkable. "There are numerous advantages to engaging in the practice of lucid dreaming, and the following are a few noteworthy examples:

Stress relief

Lucid dreaming possesses considerable advantages for alleviating stress as it enables the redirection of cognitive focus towards a realm of serene and exhilarating relaxation, while concurrently granting control over stressors that manifest in one's waking existence. Lucid dreaming offers an effective means to conquer anxiety, thereby alleviating the root cause of stress. It promotes a state of heightened relaxation and provides the opportunity to embark on captivating adventures.

Overcome fears

Lucid dreaming presents a favorable avenue for individuals to confront and conquer their apprehensions. One may utilize lucid dreams as a technique to confront and overcome their phobias by intentionally creating scenarios that represent the worst possible outcome. This deliberate approach allows the mind to recognize its capability to successfully navigate such challenging situations. Individuals who experience apprehension in high elevations may potentially exhibit behavior exceeding conventional expectations by willing to plunge from the loftiest structure within the scope of their imagination. Remarkably impervious to perils, this endeavor enables one to manipulate the perception of time, regulate the descent, and gracefully descend to the earth's surface. It revolves around the ability to confront and conquer one's greatest fears.

Learn new skills

By means of lucid dreaming, individuals are immersed in a variety of captivating experiences. This expands one's opportunities to explore and acquire skills that were previously inaccessible within their real-life circumstances. Furthermore, it is widely held that individuals who engage in occupations involving a distinct set of specific activities are able to replicate those actions within their lucid dreams, exemplified by the profession of surgeons. This will reinforce genuine actions within the brain, rendering them more instinctive and integrated into everyday life.

Explore inner creative potential

Conscious dreaming entails a potent and efficacious means by which individuals can enhance their creative capacities. In the state of lucid dreaming, there exists a consistent stream of uninhibited thoughts, which those who have encountered it tend to describe as both enjoyable and captivating. The adventurous nature of this endeavor has fostered a considerable amount of creative ingenuity. In the realm of lucid dreaming, all that you have deemed impossible in your waking thoughts can invariably be explicated. There is always an opportunity for individuals to visit a particular location that serves as a source of inspiration, allowing them to immerse themselves in their passions such as painting, photography, and other activities they deeply enjoy.

Improves memory

Lucid dreaming presents a unique occasion for individuals to consolidate the knowledge acquired throughout the day while simultaneously enriching their imaginative faculties, thereby augmenting their cognitive retention. The mere capacity to recall one's dreams and actively regulate them mentally is sufficient to enhance an individual's memory. All occurrences within a dream are a phenomenon of cognitive manipulation, and when this manipulation functions at such a pace, it becomes rejuvenated. All dormant memories persist within your brain, untouched by time, and irrespective of their buried depths. During the state of lucid dreaming, the capacity to unearth and relive these forgotten memories is heightened, greatly enhancing your ability to recall.

Creative

Numerous individuals consistently exhibit exceptional creativity in their lucid dreams, prompting artists to utilize such dreams as a valuable resource for generating practical ideas. Additionally, one does not need to possess artistic skills in order to partake in the profound creativity inherent in lucid dreaming. The mind and brain of any individual possess the capacity to forge captivating associations on a subconscious plane, which can subsequently be seamlessly integrated into their daily existence.

Get life changing information

In the context of a vivid dream, there are numerous aspects that can at times appear incredulous. There exists a subset of individuals who attain transformative knowledge solely through the state of conscious dreaming. One might, for instance, possess certain advantageous notions that have remained confined within, outstanding recollections, or even latent aptitudes. Upon delving into the depths of their subconscious through the medium of a clear and vivid dream, a multitude of revelations and unexplored aspects will invariably be unveiled. In the realm of lucid dreaming, individuals often embark on a profound exploration of their innermost being, a process that borders on the mystical, as our true nature remains largely elusive. The revelations one unearths through lucidity can indeed have a transformative impact on one's life. It is consistently a beneficial means of personal realization. When an individual engages in the state of lucid dreaming, they establish a direct connection with their subconscious mind and obtain a wealth of insights in response to numerous inquiries.

Build confidence

The concept of confronting and conquering all of your fears within the realm of a lucid dream invariably leads to the attainment of absolute self-mastery, and, perhaps most significantly, the restoration of one's self-assurance. One may utilize lucid dreaming as a means to confront and overcome personal inhibitions, thereby attaining a state of unrestrained freedom in reality, characterized by a heightened sense of self-worth and self-appreciation. If individuals encounter challenges with their speech, they can engage in deliberate practice within their lucid dreams, which subsequently facilitates the transfer of skills to the waking world. Through consistent effort and investment of time, significant enhancements in speech can be observed. Allow your vivid dream state to serve as a platform for conducting experiments, wherein you can practice tasks that pose difficulty for you in the physical realm.

It is fun

The allure of lucid dreaming lies in the enjoyment it offers, which entices numerous individuals to acquire the skills and knowledge associated with this practice. The level of power and control one attains is unparalleled, rendering the adventure it presents virtually unattainable in reality. Throughout our lives, each of us inevitably harbors desires, fantasies, and wishes that remain unfulfilled in reality. However, in the state of lucid dreaming, all of those desires can be completely gratified. This is precisely why lucid dreaming captivates individuals who have had the opportunity to partake in it. The encounter consistently provides an extraordinary and daring experience, characterized by an environment ensuring complete safety and control. There exists boundless capacity for individuals to manifest any conceivable scenario of their dreams. It is possible for individuals to engage in activities such as flying, exploring outer space, and realizing their every imagined endeavor.

Better sleep

Numerous sleep disturbances often stem from heightened levels of stress and anxiety. By engaging in the practice of lucid dreaming, individuals can effectively address the various concerns that give rise to stress and anxiety, as they immerse themselves in extraordinary experiences throughout their nights. These elements will instill a sense of anticipation, fostering a continuous eagerness to retire for the night. Nightmares invariably yield devastating effects, whereas in lucid dreams, individuals confront these fears with the assurance of their complete safety.

How to Enhance Dream Recall Upon Awakening

A multitude of individuals regard dreams as reflections and discernments pertaining to our emotions and existence. The issue at hand is that a considerable number of individuals struggle to recollect their dreams. By applying deliberate exertion and employing certain methodologies, we can facilitate the enhancement of our ability to remember our dreams with greater clarity and detail.

Ensure that you have a notepad, writing utensil such as a pencil or pen, in close proximity to your bed. These tools may be employed to promptly document your dreams upon awakening. Prior to retiring for the night, make sure to ascertain that you possess an immaculate writing surface. You may also consider employing a recording device as a viable substitute. In the event that you engage in somniloquy, you may choose to orally narrate your dream.

Focus on recalling your dreams – normally, a person can only remember the last part of their dream as soon as they wake up. It is more advisable to refrain from taking any action and remain in the initial position in which you woke up. Make an effort to recollect as many details as possible. If feasible, endeavor to contemplate every aspect from inception to conclusion. Whilst attempting to recollect, direct your concentration towards the initial visual stimulus. That particular entity will predominantly harbor the remembrance of your dream.

It is advisable to maintain a detailed record of your dreams by documenting them in a dream diary or journal, ensuring that you meticulously note down all the intricate particulars of your dream experience. Commence by constructing a rudimentary outline comprising essential elements such as the dream's backdrop, its narrative arc, the individuals encountered in the dream, and the prevailing emotion that transpired within it. Any recollections of images that you can summon would be beneficial. In the event that you can recollect any conversation, it would be advisable to transcribe it initially, given that it is typically the most susceptible to being inadvertently overlooked.

If you are unable to recollect any specific details, make a habit of swiftly recording the initial thought that enters your mind immediately after awakening. It could potentially elicit the process of memory retrieval or bear some relevance to your dream. The sentiments that materialize in your dream typically endure for a short duration upon awakening and may subsequently prompt recollection of dream events.

Increase the frequency of nocturnal awakenings as a means to augment the occurrence of dream states. It is common for us to experience multiple cycles of REM (Rapid Eye Movement) during the night, which become more extended as the morning approaches. It can be alluring to return to slumber upon awakening in the nocturnal hours, yet this juncture presents the opportune time to recollect the contents of your dreams. The act of documenting the most recent dream experienced upon awakening in the morning could result in the loss of the majority of one's overall dream sequence. Frequently rousing from sleep during the night will facilitate the prompt recollection of your dream.

You have the option to configure your alarm clock to rouse you at various intervals, such as 4, 5, or 6 hours. Typically, the dreams experienced in the latter stages of the night tend to be of extended duration.

On certain occasions, it is possible to evoke a memory by assuming the same posture one held during a dream. Attempt to recline in the identical manner by positioning your head upon the pillow at its designated location and contemplate your envisioned aspiration as your eyelids gradually close. To replicate the room's environment, it would be advisable to switch off the lights and reduce ambient noise levels.

Observe certain recurring configurations - endeavor to discern patterns, such as the hour at which you retired for the night and the hour at which you emerged from slumber. Ultimately, you will be able to discern the elements that contribute to the recollection of your dreams. You may also observe certain factors that have had an impact on your ability to recollect your dreams.

Persevere in your practice, for the ability to recall dreams necessitates both dedicated effort and repeated practice. One is more prone to recall them when one gains greater awareness of their dreams. Develop the practice and dedication to recall your nocturnal dreams consistently and promptly transcribe them upon waking. Over time, you will become accustomed to the procedure.

There is a potential for you to encounter auditory or visual stimuli later in the day that bear relevance to the content of your dream. "This can potentially stimulate your memory and aid in recollection." Additionally, it is advantageous to consistently keep one's aspirations at the forefront of one's thoughts throughout the day.

Correlations between Lucid Dreaming and Related Experiences

Lucid dreaming may be correlated with additional nocturnal occurrences. These phenomena have the potential to elicit lucid dreams or are interconnected. Out of body experiences, also known as OBEs or OOBEs, entail the vivid perception of one's consciousness detaching from the physical vessel. Occasionally, extending well beyond that, it empowers an individual to embark on a journey. This occurrence is more probable when an individual is in a state of slumber, engaging in the practice of the WILD technique (Wake-Induced Lucid Dream), or partaking in meditation. Dream authorities concur that this astral projection occurrence is indeed a component of the lucid dreaming phenomenon. Certain individuals may encounter these occurrences with greater frequency. There exist numerous techniques to provoke an out-of-body experience (OBE).

The Correlation between Out of Body Experiences and Lucid Dreaming

Based on substantial scientific evidence, it can be concluded that Out-of-Body Experiences (OBEs) bear considerable resemblance to the phenomenon of lucid dreaming. The methods used to induce out-of-body experiences bear a striking resemblance to those employed in the Wake Induced Lucid Dream state. Essentially, they are identical occurrences: "In effect, they are indistinguishable phenomena: "Fundamentally, they are equivalent phenomena: "Essentially, they are synonymous phenomena: "Practically speaking, they are interchangeable phenomena: "In essence, they are analogous phenomena:

Both OBE and WILD are initiated when one is reclining or has recently awakened. Our physical being reverts to a state of sleep paralysis and subsequently enters into a state of slumber. Nevertheless, you remain cognizant unlike during conventional sleep. This phenomenon may induce an atypical sensation of confinement within one's physical form, contrasting with an innate desire for liberation. The phenomenon of experiencing a lucid dream occurs when individuals maintain an active state of consciousness during the dream state.

Lucid dreamers assert that the encounter can be exceedingly vivid and remarkably lifelike. Almost every night, we have dreams and undergo out-of-body experiences unknowingly. On each occasion we embark on a journey within our dream state, we have a propensity to autonomously traverse our surroundings, wholly detached from our corporeal vessel resting in bed. Out-of-body experience (OBE) denotes a state in which one's consciousness transcends the physical confines of the body, without necessarily implying a literal physical detachment during nocturnal hours.

What distinguishes the phenomenon of OBE from a standard dream?

The individual exhibits a heightened state of consciousness and perceptiveness throughout the encounter.

You enhance the experience by transcending your corporeal form

Methods to Engage in Out-of-Body Experiences:

Attain a state of physical and mental relaxation. Inhale deeply and exhale slowly while reclining in a comfortable position. Make an effort to refrain from dwelling on other matters and allow your eyelids to gently and spontaneously shut.

Begin your meditation routine. Eliminate any sources of distraction and strive to maintain concentration and mental clarity as you transition into sleep.

Direct your attention away from your physical form and endeavor to mentally envision geometric patterns. This phenomenon is alternatively referred to as consciously entering a state of sleep. You might experience the onset of sleep paralysis abruptly. Permit it to be so, as you approach a state of encountering an out-of-body experience.

It is possible that you could experience a sensation of weightlessness, however, rest assured that your physical body remains reclined in your bed.

False awakenings can be a perplexing occurrence for individuals engaged in both conscious dreaming and unaware dreaming. They were genuinely persuaded that they had awoken and were actively engaging in authentic existence. This phenomenon is commonly observed when individuals experience heightened anticipation for an upcoming significant event, or in the case of individuals who possess the ability to consciously control their dreams. The level of your self-awareness delineates the extent to which you are consciously attuned to the present state of affairs. Individuals who possess the ability to experience lucid dreams tend to exhibit a heightened sense of self-awareness in both their waking state and during their dream state.

Certain individuals may encounter a phenomenon characterized by a succession of recurrent false awakenings, wherein they repetitively perform identical tasks without an accurate perception of their true state of wakefulness. Subsequently, you will commence undertaking more challenging undertakings within your dream, consequently stimulating the conscious segment of your brain to rouse from slumber. Individuals who possess the ability to consciously control their dreams, referred to as lucid dreamers, experience a greater frequency of deceptive awakenings within the realm of their unconsciousness compared to those who do not possess this capability. This presents a favorable occasion for them to gain additional structured aspirations. It may prove challenging to ascertain instances of false awakenings, however, through dedicated practice and refinement of discernment, one can enhance their aptitude in recognizing these occurrences.

Sleep Paralysis

Sleep paralysis serves as a inherent safeguard that inhibits us from physically manifesting actions from our dreams. It exerts an influence on the majority of our physique, with the exception of the ocular organs, enabling the manifestation of Rapid Eye Movement, the pulmonary system to respire, and selected appendages. It transitions between an active and inactive state, with occasional instances where individuals become conscious of this dynamic and are startled by their inability to mobilize. This may evoke fear in others. The duration of this experience can range from a few seconds to several minutes.

Sleep paralysis refers to a condition in which the physical body is immobilized during the onset of sleep or upon awakening. Disruptions to one's sleep schedule and insufficient sleep have the potential to result in the occurrence of sleep paralysis. This phenomenon can also be observed in narcolepsy, a medical condition distinguished by heightened somnolence throughout daylight hours. Sleep paralysis does not inherently pose any detrimental risks, however, individuals encountering this phenomenon often harbor a sense of fear due to a lack of comprehension regarding the experience.

The fundamental factor behind sleep paralysis is the occurrence of REM atonia, an inherent phenomenon that can manifest in individuals universally and is regarded as a significant mechanism of sleep. Atonia refers to the absence of muscular tension. The phenomenon manifests itself when a fragment of the consciousness is alert, while the physical body remains in a state of slumber. You are in a state of mental awareness while simultaneously being physically in a state of sleep, rendering your body seemingly immobilized.

Benefits Of Lucid Dreaming

Consciously engaging in the act of dreaming holds significant potential in enhancing an individual's creativity. By means of lucid dreaming, individuals demonstrate their utmost creativity, stemming from the unrestrained generation of ideas originating from the subconscious. In the realm of lucid dreaming, individuals have the opportunity to venture into realms previously deemed unattainable. This facilitates the unlocking of an aspect of their identity and enables the discovery of the most captivating endeavors. In the state of lucid dreaming, individuals intentionally immerse themselves in a realm of inspiration related to their passions, such as the art of painting.

(b.) Obtain transformative knowledge
By means of engaging in lucid dreaming, individuals have the capability to immerse themselves in transformative

experiences that can profoundly impact their lives. It is conceivable that individuals possess unexpressed contemplations, cherished recollections, and latent abilities. Lucid dreaming provides individuals with the capacity to delve into profound introspection and acquire transformative insights.

(c.) Confront fears
There exist individuals who employ their lucid dreams as a means to actively surmount their apprehensions. This can be achieved by intentionally arranging one's lucid dream to encounter specific perilous or disconcerting scenarios, from which one ultimately attains the knowledge that they possess dominion over or will successfully overcome. The more they progressively reconcile with their fears, the more expeditiously they will develop the aptitude to address those fears.

(d.) A chance to hone one's skills
Lucid dreams consistently offer a plethora of intriguing experiences for

individuals. Thus, it enables them to uncover new abilities that would have otherwise remained undiscovered in the physical realm. Numerous individuals, whose occupational success hinges upon their aptitude to execute precise actions, dedicate themselves to honing their proficiency through the practice of lucid dreaming. Examples of such professionals encompass pilots and surgeons, among others.

(e.) Stress relief
One of the most advantageous aspects of lucid dreaming is its efficacy as a potent mechanism for alleviating stress. When experiencing heightened levels of stress, individuals may embark upon captivating expeditions within the realm of lucid dreaming. This will facilitate the amplification of mental and physical relaxation. In the state of lucid dreaming, individuals possess the capacity to exert control, enabling them to modify any unfolding scenario within their dream to align with their preferences.

(f.) Aptitude for resolving issues (f.) Proficiency in troubleshooting (f.) Ability to effectively address challenges (f.) Competence in resolving complex problems (f.) Proficient problem-solving abilities

Clarity of thought is widely recognized as highly beneficial for effective problem-solving. This advantage is widely recognized by scientists and mathematicians. During the state of lucid dreaming, the cognitive faculties undergo alterations, thereby enabling profound contemplation on matters within the realm of one's dreams. The intellect provides individuals with associations and insights that may not have been considered otherwise. They have the opportunity to experiment with various approaches to resolve interpersonal challenges and observe the outcomes.

An 8-Step Guide to Attaining Expertise in Lucid Dreaming

As previously elucidated, a lucid dream pertains to the state of dreaming in which one possesses an awareness of the dream's nature and exercises complete mastery of its content. Lucid dreaming has been a prevailing practice believed to have existed since the earliest stages of human civilization. The initial recorded instance of the practice of lucid dreaming can be traced back to the year 415A. St. Augustine articulated that during sleep, the physical body may be in a state of slumber while the mind, residing within the confines of the brain, remains fully conscious and alert, actively engaging with the subjective reality it constructs. This state of heightened awareness within the realm of the mind facilitates the experience of lucid dreaming. Although it may require a considerable amount of practice, with perseverance, anyone can attain it.

Once an individual achieves the ability to engage in lucid dreaming, it can prove to be a highly intriguing phenomenon that ought to be harnessed to one's own benefit. The primary fundamental approach to achieving lucid dreams is for individuals to possess a comprehensive comprehension of its nature and practical applications. One cannot attain the ability to experience lucid dreams unless one possesses a comprehensive understanding of its nature and distinguishing features from ordinary dreams. The delight of lucid dreams lies in the absolute control one possesses; individuals become the ultimate authority over their dreams, enabling them to manifest their every desire. There are no terrestrial constraints, thereby endowing them with the capability to achieve flight, engage in creative endeavors, and so forth. It provides a platform for individuals to articulate and pursue their heartfelt aspirations, actions that may potentially disrupt affairs if enacted in the realm of reality. They have the opportunity to articulate and delve into the realm of what is deemed unattainable. These dreams occasionally exhibit such a high degree of realism that they diminish the sensation of being grounded in physical reality. There exist individuals who encounter difficulties in experiencing lucid dreams, thus I have assembled a meticulously crafted manual consisting of eight sequential stages, aiming to facilitate the realization and mastery of the realm of lucid dreaming.

Step 1: Meditation

The practice of meditation for the purpose of inducing lucid dreaming yields considerable advantages. It constitutes a component of both mnemonic induction of lucid dreams and wake-induced lucid dreams, effectively enhancing lucidity. This phenomenon can be described as a silent dialogue between the soul and the inner self. Meditation offers a multitude of advantages and favorable outcomes for both the mind and body. The concept underlying meditation involves the ability to channel one's cognitive resources towards a particular objective, thus facilitating the attainment of one's aspirations. The correlation between meditation and lucid dreaming lies in their shared capacity to foster heightened self-awareness and introspection.

The practice of meditation is employed to induce lucid dreaming, as it enhances an individual's aptitude for dream, recall, visualization, and the capacity to achieve lucidity. Consistent practice of meditation facilitates the attainment of complete relaxation, consequently enhancing the likelihood of experiencing lucid dreams. It is crucial to recognize the significance of engaging in meditation and comprehend that it is a practice that enhances one's capacity for self-control. Meditation is intricately linked to the notion of consciousness, which constitutes the essence of lucid dreaming.

Meditation is purported to bolster lucid dreaming by augmenting the following aspects:

- Relaxation.

- Stress relief.

- Self-awareness.

- Enhances abstract thought.

- Concentration.

Meditation is constituted by three sequential stages that are efficacious in achieving lucid dreaming. The aforementioned elements encompass relaxation, focus, and a state of open awareness. Engaging in relaxation techniques facilitates the physical readiness for sleep, while maintaining concentration aids in preserving mental alertness or stabilizing the dream state, and open focus serves to enhance awareness during the lucid state. This will contribute to the extension and preservation of a state of heightened awareness during a dream. The cultivation of concentration, mindfulness, and attentiveness are pivotal factors in attaining the state of lucid dreaming.

Process of meditating:

(i.) Assume a seated posture that is comfortable, and if you choose to adopt a crossed-leg position.

(ii.) Reside in a setting where you have the ability to minimize all types of disruptions to facilitate focus.

(iii.) Permit the lids of your eyes to gently descend while directing your attention towards the rhythm of your breath.

(iv.) Engage in deep inhalation and exhalation, while actively maintaining mindfulness of your breath.

To circumvent the proliferation of disorganized thoughts within one's mind, it is advisable to maintain concentration on one's breath, thereby facilitating the consolidation of thoughts and the subsequent purification of one's mental faculties.

(verb) Engage in this activity for approximately 10 to 15 minutes in order to attain a state of tranquility in your mind.

(vii.) By doing so, you will subsequently attain a state of mental clarity and serenity.

Second Step: Enhancing the Ability to Remember Dreams

Enhancing the ability to remember dreams is a fundamental approach for individuals seeking to achieve and sustain lucid dreaming states. It is imperative to note that in order to experience lucid dreaming, it is crucial to possess the ability to recall at least one vivid dream on a nightly basis. This is attributed to its capacity to enhance an individual's self-awareness. It has been postulated that the act of recalling dreams serves as the initial stage towards achieving lucidity in dreams. If an individual is unable to recall their regular dreams, it will pose a challenge for them to recollect their lucid dreams when they experience them. The key to enhancing dream recollection lies in ensuring an ample amount of rest. There are several strategies that individuals can employ to improve their ability to recall dreams.

(a.) Meditation

The practice of meditation facilitates the development of enhanced self-awareness, thereby facilitating effortless recollection of dreams. Engaging in meditation shortly before bedtime can be highly effective, as it prepares the mind for enhanced cognitive introspection by inducing relaxation and facilitating focused concentration.

(b.) Maintaining a journal to record one's dreams

Maintaining a dream journal can significantly aid in the recollection of dreams. Prior to retiring for the night, it is essential to make certain that a writing instrument, such as a pen or pencil, is readily accessible on the bedside table. Alternatively, a digital recorder may also serve as a viable alternative. When one awakens during the night with a captivating dream, endeavor to document it. By consistently recording your dreams, you will eventually develop the ability to discern recurring events or symbols. Furthermore, this method serves as a commendable approach to dissecting and interpreting one's dreams.

Consume a glass of water prior to retiring for the night.

Consuming water prior to bedtime is a convenient method to regulate one's body's inherent equilibrium. It will enhance the probability of awakening upon completion of a dreaming cycle. When an individual can awaken near the conclusion of a dream, it is likely that the dream will remain vivid in their memory. The sensation of a distended urinary bladder has the ability to stimulate cognitive awareness towards the conclusion of a dream.

(d.) Dream supplements

Dream supplements encompass herbal remedies consumed with the intent of enhancing dream vividness. The sole potential adverse consequence is an augmented ability to recollect dreams. There exist certain botanical remedies, such as Calea Zacatechichi, as well as dietary supplements, like vitamin B6, that have the capability to elicit enhanced dreaming experiences characterized by heightened self-awareness. Upon awakening in the morning, individuals often experience vivid dreams that occasionally lead to lucid dreaming.

(e.) Allocate dedicated periods for Rapid Eye Movement (REM) sleep.

Engaging in morning Rapid Eye Movement sleep can effectively amplify the ability to recall dreams. Prior to entering REM sleep, it is crucial to ensure an adequate amount of sleep, approximately 8 hours, as the attainment of mental clarity and alertness relies on a mind that is both relaxed and fully rested.

(f.) Enough sleep

Obtaining an ample or sufficient amount of sleep is a factor contributing to the enhancement of dream recollection. An advantage of obtaining sufficient rest is that the duration and frequency of dreams intensify progressively throughout the night.

Step 3: Reality check

Engaging in reality checks is of significant importance in the attainment of lucid dreams. They exemplify a straightforward method for achieving lucid dreaming, which enhances one's self-awareness and enables individuals to explore their subconscious realms during the nocturnal hours. Reality checks are methodologies employed to ascertain one's state of wakefulness. In order for individuals to acquire proficiency in lucid dreaming, it is imperative that they possess the capability to discern and distinguish between the realm of dreams and the actuality of their waking life. To detect the presence of a dream state, individuals may employ reality check inquiries or behaviors. There exists a multitude of reality checks designed for the identification of lucid dreams.

Example:

1.) Respiration: Is it possible to obstruct the flow of air to your nose and mouth and yet continue to engage in breathing?

2.) Hand Palms: Are the palm regions of your hand appearing normal upon close examination?

3.) Visual acuity: Is your visual acuity heightened or impaired compared to your usual state?

4.) Leap: upon leaping, do you descend gracefully?

5.) Hand: Is it possible to penetrate a solid surface with your hand?

Gaining expertise in the application of reality checks is a crucial milestone. It will assist individuals in discerning between states of dreaming and wakefulness. It is typically challenging to remember to engage in the practice of reality checks, thus it is recommended to cultivate the habit of performing reality checks in real-world situations. By employing reality checks, individuals grant themselves a pause for reflection, granting them the chance for contemplation. It is recommended that individuals engage in reality checks whenever they recall to do so, and it is advisable to incorporate a minimum of 2 to 3 reality checks simultaneously into their practice.

Step 4: Visualization

Visualization serves as a means of augmenting the clarity and vividness of one's dreams. It is most effectively executed when an individual is in a state of profound relaxation and experiences a strong inclination towards falling asleep effortlessly. An individual can employ the technique of mentally picturing subjects that captivate their curiosity in order to foster a pathway towards attaining the state of lucid dreaming. By means of this mechanism, individuals can gradually attain regulated dreaming. A set of prescribed procedures must be followed in order to attain complete visualization.

1.) Visualization: This step involves conjuring an image in your mind as a conscious mental representation.

2.) Hypnagogia: By attaining a state of bodily relaxation and closing your eyes, your brain will gradually guide you towards sleep, inducing the hypnagogic state. In this particular juncture, one may experience an ascending perception, such as the amplification of auditory nuances and kinesthetic motions. This is the condition in which you have the opportunity to enhance the realism of your visualization.

3.) Wake initiated lucid dreams: In this state, the physical body enters a state of sleep while the conscious mind assumes control over the dream's visualization, enhancing its realism.

Please take note that optimal opportunities for attempting visualization techniques arise in the middle of the night upon awakening, early in the morning while still experiencing fatigue, and also during an afternoon repose.

Step 5: Self-hypnosis

Self-induced hypnosis serves as a potent means of facilitating the occurrence of lucid dreams. Similar to the practice of meditation, it enables individuals to attain a state of tranquility which promotes the soothing of the mind and body, ultimately enhancing concentration on specific thoughts. Self-hypnosis employs the technique of employing suggestions to beget targeted thoughts.

To facilitate the experience of lucid dreaming, it is valuable to employ affirmations such as "I am capable of recalling my dreams" and similar statements. It is thus imperative in the realm of lucid dreaming, as it facilitates the recollection of dreams, enables their intentional shaping or direction, and fosters heightened self-awareness.

Hypnosis is the process of inducing a state of relaxation in the individual's brain. It bestows individuals with the capacity to seek guidance from their subconscious and establish a connection with their inner psyche.

Process:

1.) The initial stage involves attaining a comfortable position, either by sitting or lying down, while avoiding the crossing of legs or arms. Please allow your eyes to gently close and take three deliberate and unhurried breaths. Carefully process and evaluate the multitude of thoughts that arise within your consciousness, and then let them go.

2.) The subsequent phase entails directing your attention towards alleviating physical tension across your entire body through the use of visualization techniques aimed at inducing relaxation in each individual muscle.

3.) The third procedure entails mentally envisioning yourself descending a staircase and gradually deepening your state of relaxation as you continue with your descent.

4.) Upon reaching the lowermost step of the staircase, you may commence the process of auto-suggestion, exemplified by...

I possess the ability to recall and recollect my dreams.

- "I possess the ability to experience lucid dreams." • "It is within my capacity to engage in lucid dreaming." • "I am capable of entering into a state of lucid dreaming." • "I have the capability to achieve lucidity during my dreams."

- "I am able to attain lucidity within the realm of my dreams."

- "I have the ability to manipulate and govern the content of my dreams." • "I possess the capacity to exercise control over the narrative and events within my dreams." • "I am capable of regulating and steering the course of my dreams."

Throughout the process of hypnosis, each inhalation imbues the body with a soothing and calming energy.

Step 6: Lucid affirmations

An affirmation consists of a definitive declaration that an individual imparts to their subconscious mind, conveying their desired outcome. This technique is highly applicable to the practice of lucid dreaming, as individuals can effectively instruct their subconscious mind to serve as a prompt for recognizing their own dreams, a task it successfully fulfills.

Individuals may engage in the practice of making deliberate, clear affirmations while reclining in bed, affirming within themselves the intention to attain a state of lucidity in their dreams. This process is performed iteratively until the subconscious mind becomes fatigued by its repetition.

The coherent assertions ought to facilitate the recognition within the subconscious realm regarding the state of being in a dream, enabling individuals to exert authority over the entirety of their dream experience.

Seventh Step: Utilizing Herbal Remedies and Supplements

Lucid dreaming is an inherent phenomenon; however, there exist individuals who are unable to spontaneously engage in this state. Certain dietary supplements and herbal remedies have shown potential in facilitating the experience of lucid dreaming with relative ease. "These offer assistance by performing the following functions: "These provide support by carrying out the following actions: "These aid individuals by accomplishing the following tasks: "These assist individuals by executing the following activities: "These contribute to helping individuals by undertaking the following actions:

• Enhancing dream recall.

• Facilitating the development of self-awareness in individuals.

• Enhancing the depth of your sleep. • Augmenting the quality of your sleep. • Elevating the level of your sleep's intensity. • Amplifying the profoundness of your sleep.

- Offer assistance in providing significance to your dreams.
- Aid in bestowing interpretation upon your dreams.
- Provide support in ascertaining the meaning behind your dreams.
- Assist in unraveling the significance concealed within your dreams.
- Offer guidance in elucidating the symbolism embedded within your dreams.

- Facilitates the maintenance of vivid dreams, as well as the occurrence of lucid dreams.

Here are some illustrations of the herbs and supplements that can be utilized for the purpose of establishing lucid dreaming.

- Calea Zacatechichi induces extremely lucid dreaming experiences.

- Galantamine is significantly influential in enhancing the capacity to remember dreams.

- Choline plays a crucial role in facilitating the recollection of dreams.

- Huperzine: helps in dream recall and self-awareness.

- Alpha brain nootropic: designed to enhance cognitive acuity and promote heightened mental clarity.

- Mugwort herb is utilized for the purpose of enhancing dream recall.

Step 8: WBTB method

The "re-entering sleep technique" is a simple approach for individuals to acquire the skill of lucid dreaming. It functions effortlessly as it involves the activation of the conscious mind during the customary period of REM sleep, resulting in the manifestation of consciousness within dreams.

Process:

First, adhere to your regular bedtime routine and subsequently rest for a duration of 6 hours. Please ensure that you set an alarm or arrange for someone to rouse you.

Secondly, once the aforementioned duration of 6 hours has elapsed, proceed to disembark from your resting place and awaken yourself completely. Engage in an activity that will heighten your state of alertness. Please remain attentive for a duration of approximately 20 to 60 minutes.

Step 3: Subsequently, you should retreat to your sleeping quarters and engage in relaxation. If your mind is still very alert do something like meditation to take your thoughts away. Subsequently, employ your cognitive abilities in visualizing as a means to guide your thoughts back towards the realm of dreams, strategically outlining the course of your lucid dream while gradually succumbing to slumber.

Key Pertinent Information regarding Lucid Dreaming

Allow me to present to you a compilation of lesser-known aspects pertaining to lucid dreaming - a remarkable phenomenon wherein one possesses the extraordinary capacity to exercise deliberate control over and maintain awareness within the realm of their dreams.

Lucid Dream Fast Fact No. 1: The initial documentation of lucid dreams can be traced back to the Ancient Egyptians.

The ancient Egyptians were a highly advanced civilization that thrived more than five millennia in the past. As per the assertions made by Jeremy Naydler, the author of the renowned work titled "The Temple of Cosmos," the ancient Egyptian culture maintained a belief in a trichotomy of entities: firstly, the soul or Ba; secondly, the animated physical body or Ka; and lastly, the mortal remains or Shat.

Ba was usually manifested in hieroglyphics as a human-headed bird flying above the sleeping corpse of body. As per Naydler's analysis, the Ba can be regarded as the individual, albeit in a different manifestation. The Ba can be described as an individual existing in a disembodied state.

Lucid Dream Fast Fact No. 2: It is estimated that approximately 20% of individuals experience lucid dreams on a monthly or more frequent basis.

Gackenback and Snyder conducted a survey in 1988, which unveiled that 20 percent of individuals purportedly encounter a lucid dream on a monthly basis, with 50 percent having experienced it at least once during their lifetimes.

This serves to illustrate that lucid dreaming is a commonplace occurrence, notwithstanding the fact that most individuals are uninformed of the precise terminology or do not deliberately induce their own lucid dreams. It seems to be quite commonplace for individuals, especially children, to possess the ability to exercise spontaneous control over their dreams.

One plausible explanation for this phenomenon is that children are particularly prone to experiencing night-time disturbances known as nightmares, which can provoke highly intense and vivid emotional responses.

This stimulates the specific region of the cerebral cortex that governs self-awareness, granting the adolescent visionary a state of lucidity conducive to recognizing their dream state.

Lucid Dream Fast Fact No. 3: Individuals engaging in lucid dreaming possess the ability to establish communication with the external reality.

In 1975, Dr. Keith Hearne, a distinguished British psychologist, accomplished a groundbreaking feat - he successfully documented the ocular motions of an individual while he was immersed in a state of slumber and actively participating in a lucid dream.

Crucially, these two individuals had reached a mutual consensus on a predetermined arrangement of visual cues. Through the deliberate movement of his gaze within a state of conscious dreaming, the individual was able to establish a means of communication with Dr. Hearne in the external realm.

This groundbreaking research has substantiated, for the initial instance, the authenticity of consciousness within the realm of dreams.

Lucid Dream Fast Fact No. 4: Lucid dreams originate from a distinct region within the neural architecture of the brain.

J Allan Hobson, a respected neuroscientist, has posited upon the cognitive processes taking place within the human brain during instances of lucid dreaming.

Firstly, an individual possessed of vivid imagination shall acknowledge their state of being in a dream. This will elicit activation of the dorsolateral prefrontal cortex, which governs self-awareness and the cognitive processes associated with working memory. During REM sleep, it is customary for this particular area of the brain to undergo deactivation. Consequently, it is uncommon for us to possess the ability to perceive our dreams or effortlessly recollect their intricacies.

Upon the onset of clarity, the dreamer shall delicately navigate the threshold between maintaining slumber and retaining awareness, albeit to a sufficient extent to recollect their state of being within a dream.

Surprisingly, the dorsalateral prefrontal cortex exhibits distinctive neural connections that are specifically intertwined with the subjective perception of determining the appropriate course of action and its timing.

Potential Hypotheses: Exploring Strategies for Overcoming Nocturnal Palsy Through the Induction of Illusory Movement

There exist multiple potential, albeit purely speculative, rationales for this phenomenon. Upon observation, I observed that upon witnessing my projection into the astral body, I subsequently regained consciousness within said physical form. Please be aware that information is no longer retained in the astral body at the commencement of the designated time frame.

The state of unconsciousness. The deprivation of consciousness cannot be accounted for by the departure of the astral entity from the corporeal form. The astral body has the ability to exist in a state of consciousness separate from the physical body, as well as in a state of unconsciousness. Additionally, it can also be unconscious while residing within the physical body. While the loss of knowledge and the departure of the astral body are distinct phenomena, they typically tend to manifest simultaneously. The existence of conscious astral projection would be rendered impossible if the act of the astral body departing the physical realm resulted in loss of consciousness. Entering a state of trance (prior to falling asleep) inherently transitions one into a state of restfulness, whereby the astral body becomes marginally detached by a mere quarter of an inch, enabling the retention of consciousness and subsequent encounter of reverberations. This happens very often. The celestial entity transitions into a state of repose mere instants prior to the cessation of consciousness. As a result, numerous occultists came to conjecture that the state of unconsciousness can be attributed to the departure of the astral body. However, this constitutes an error.

It is additionally accurate to assert that we may experience a state of unconsciousness in our physical form prior to the arrival of the astral body into the state of repose. It is applicable in instances where the body is influenced by some form of stimulant. However, these situations are rare occurrences. Generally speaking, once consciousness is switched off, it is customary for the astral body to promptly separate from the physical body. This phenomenon demonstrates rapid progression in certain individuals while for others, it varies based on the individual's state of health. It can be comprehended that achieving conscious projection requires the prior transition to the state of rest, which entails the subsequent shutdown of consciousness. This condition is determined by numerous contributing factors, including temperament, physical inaction, and other aspects, as previously discussed.

If consciousness ultimately departs from us when the astral body enters an unconscious state, then it follows that knowledge must be partially disassociated from the aggregate while the latter retains some degree of consciousness. When the individual experiences a dream wherein they perceive the motion of their astral form and subsequently attains entry into it, there exists the possibility that the extracted portion of their consciousness operated within a conceptual framework such as this. Alternatively, it is possible that within this dream state, a more nuanced form, aligned with the astral body, dissociated from it and observed its actions before subsequently reuniting with it.

The optimal approach to induce the required level of "stress" in the subconscious mind would be to strategically activate the projection through mental stimulation. Why not cultivate a habit unrelated to screening that exerts subconscious influence, while opting to develop a direct inclination towards projection, thereby enabling one to perceive dreams that align seamlessly with actual reality instead of relying on an indirect habitual approach?

Regular Practice of Meditation is Recommended

Meditation ought to be performed for a duration of 5 to 10 minutes, on a daily basis, in order to achieve swift and efficient results. Adhere to the prescribed rules and guidelines at all times.

And the inclusion of its diverse array of strengths is necessary for achieving a sense of equilibrium in your abilities. When one possesses the requisite electrical energy, a harmonious equilibrium is achieved among the various chakras, enabling the ability to project oneself astrally with utmost proficiency.

False Awakening

This phenomenon is commonly perceived as resembling Lucid Dreaming, however, it must be clarified that it does not truly constitute Lucid Dreaming. In this particular dream scenario, the person 'regains consciousness' only to discover that they are in an environment resembling, if not identical to, the room where they originally retired for the night. Frequently, individuals commence their customary morning regimen, only to have it disrupted upon awakening once more. This interruption may manifest as yet another deceptive awakening or as a genuine occurrence. At this juncture, the state of consciousness ensues, prompting the individual to perceive their prior experience as a dream. The astral body, an inherent component within each individual, represents a precise replica of one's physical embodiment. It comprises of ethereal matter of a delicate nature and is typically encompassed within a corporeal form. Under normal circumstances, the detachment of the astral body from its physical counterpart is a task of considerable challenge. However, in the context of dreams, significant psychological strain alongside specific circumstances of paranormal advancement could result in the astral form being liberated and embarking upon an extensive expedition, traversing at a velocity surpassed only by that of light waves. During such journeys, a continuous and slender thread establishes a connection between the astral form and the corporal vessel. In the event of a malfunction, immediate fatality can occur, although such instances remain exceedingly rare in actuality. The ethereal form persists for a considerable duration following the demise of the corporeal vessel, albeit gradually undergoing decomposition as time passes. On occasion, it lingers in the proximity of the interment site of the corporeal remains, leading to misconceptions regarding its status as the ethereal manifestation of the departed individual. Indeed, it is merely a hollow or more delicate vessel for the essence of one's being.

The ethereal form of the deceased frequently manifests in the company of companions and close acquaintances shortly prior to the termination of their physical existence - a phenomenon arising from the intense longing of the deceased to witness and be perceptible. During psychopathic phenomena, it is not uncommon for the astral body to dissociate from its physical counterpart and venture to remote locations, sensing some sort of occurrence transpiring there. Additionally, it exits the physical form during what are commonly referred to as psychosomatic dreams, either induced by the administration of pain medication or during more profound states of hypnosis. Subsequently, it explores unfamiliar landscapes and locations, engaging in discourse with other celestial entities or disembodied beings on occasion. The brain, due to inadequate training and development, is responsible for fragmented and altered recollections of these dreams, resembling a tarnished or impaired photographic plate. I recognize that the reader has already established their conviction regarding the authenticity of the phenomenon or possesses a concealed inclination to embrace it. We shall refrain from engaging in a discourse on spiritualism at large as it lacks relevance to the resolution of the matter concerning astral projection. There exist scholarly works on this subject penned by authors of superior proficiency compared to myself. Within this research endeavor, our primary focus centers on the exploration of diverse atypical manifestations of astral body dynamics observed during an individual's lifetime. It is worth noting that while the astral body continues to persist beyond mortal demise, literature exists that delves into its subsequent existence. Therefore, our focus is on scrutinizing the astral form prior to its permanent detachment from its physical counterpart. We identify ourselves as possessing physical vitality, although in truth, our material existence holds no more vitality than an inanimate object. This is the fundamental force that underlies the physiological processes, rendering them truly "vital." The nerves in and of themselves do not possess life - were they living, we would have prematurely laid to rest numerous individuals. This heightened state of anxiety imbues them with vitality, and the astral body serves as a reservoir for the nervous energy which you are presently utilizing.

Facilitating the induction of lucid dreams

There exist three widely acknowledged approaches through which individuals can attain a state of Lucid Dreaming. These are.

• The Induction of Lucid Dreams through the Process of Dream Initiation (DI) • The Facilitation of Lucid Dreams via

Dream Induction Techniques (DIT) • Initiating Lucid Dreams through the Practice of Dream Induction (DILD) • The Activation of Lucid Dreams through Dream Initiation Strategies (DIS) • Facilitating the Beginning of Lucid Dreams through Dream Initiation Methods (DIM)

• The practice of inducing lucid dreams through the use of mnemonic techniques, also referred to as Mnemonic Initiation of Lucid Dreams (MILD).

• The Induction of Lucid Dreams through Waking Initiation (WILD)

DILD

This represents the most prevalent manner in which Lucid Dreams manifest and serves as the initial encounter for a significant portion of individuals with this phenomenon. The individual enters a state of natural slumber and proceeds to engage in the exploration of dreams.

Whilst experiencing the dream state, the conscious aspects of the cerebral cortex (or relevant portions) tend to elicit their usual responses, leading the dreamer to acquire a realization of their state of dreaming. These dreams are frequently marked by their ordinary essence. The occurrences of the concept will either transpire on a daily basis or, at the very least, not deviate from the norm. Certain elements of the objective may appear peculiar, or the encounter may be unfamiliar. As the individual attains the awareness of being in a state of dreaming, they commence to exhibit a certain degree of agency and thereby gain the ability to manipulate and mold the occurrences within the dream realm. The aforementioned category of Lucid Dream is likely to be encountered by the majority of individuals. Nevertheless, there is a lack of discernible methodologies for attaining the aforementioned objective. Although it is highly likely to occur at a certain point in one's life, achieving this most innate manifestation of Lucid Dreaming can be particularly challenging.

MILD

This method was first introduced and developed by Stephen LaBerge, a prominent authority in the realm of Lucid Dreaming. The approach involves instructing the mind to recognize the state of being in a dream. To our astonishment, it appears that this task is relatively straightforward. The method primarily revolves around forming a routine during your waking hours and perpetuating it during your slumber. The activity in question should thus be acknowledged as evidence that one is currently within a state of dreaming. Although the explanation may appear intricate, it is essentially straightforward. Recommended practices include the act of counting your fingers while you are conscious, preferably after settling into bed. Examine each finger attentively and endeavor to form a precise visual representation of them within your cognitive faculties. Continue to count and observe for a brief period of time, after which endeavor to attain a state of relaxation and facilitate the onset of slumber. After entering the state of slumber, the brain initiates its process of organizing and evaluating the events that occurred throughout the day. It may or may not address the latter matter initially. Nonetheless, employing this approach typically yields certain degree of achievement. The visual component of your perception holds significance in this context; within the dream realm, the fingers may exhibit an excessive or deficient count compared to what is expected. This serves as a prompt for you to recognize that you are experiencing a state of dreaming. Upon attaining an awareness, at this juncture, portions of your subconscious mind are rekindled, signifying the commencement of your ability to exercise command over the dream state. The "MILD" technique is especially advantageous for novices and can yield results in a matter of days or weeks from the acquisition of the skill.

WILD

This technique presents heightened complexity and a greater level of difficulty to attain proficiency compared to MILD, thus necessitating diligent practice. In the techniques known as DILD (Dream Induced Lucid Dreaming) and MILD (Mnemonic Induced Lucid Dreaming), individuals typically enter a state of sleep, experience dreams, and subsequently regain partial awareness. In this methodology, the objective is to maintain a heightened state of awareness as one transitions into sleep, allowing for a seamless entry into the realm of dreams. Efficient approaches to accomplish this objective involve engaging in meditation and relaxation strategies, in order to attain a state of somnolence where the mind retains partial focus and consciousness to facilitate the onset of sleep. There are certain junctures within the sleep cycle wherein this technique can prove to be of notable utility. In the event of an interruption to REM, it will promptly resume upon the onset of sleep. By intentionally rousing yourself earlier than your customary waking time and subsequently returning to slumber, or alternatively, arising and subsequently indulging in a nap later in the day, you will induce a state conducive to the rapid onset of dreaming. Integration of this approach with a method of inducing physical and mental relaxation to expedite the process of entering a Lucid Dream can prove advantageous in attaining direct entry.

Please be aware that there is a high probability of encountering sleep paralysis when employing this particular method during the process of transitioning into sleep. One may encounter a diminished capacity for mobility, a perception of descent, and peculiar visual and auditory stimuli. This phenomenon is entirely ordinary (it occurs each time we enter a state of sleep), yet typically we do not consciously perceive it in normal situations. One should be prepared for encountering a couple of unusual experiences if they engage in the application of this method.

Dual or Extra-Corporeal Encounters

The realm of our imagination possesses vast and remarkable depth, surpassing what one might initially perceive, as does the complexity of our corporeal form. It possesses clear discernment between what is beneficial and detrimental to its well-being.

In fact, it has the remarkable capacity to acclimate to any environmental circumstance, irrespective of its potential classification as perilous to life. The human physique possesses the inherent ability to effectively resolve any challenge it confronts, provided that the accompanying character instills and affirms this capability unto it. Furthermore, the human immune system possesses the ability to overcome any virus, regardless of its level of resistance.

According to medical literature, it is asserted that viruses possess the ability to deceive the human body and induce a state of illness, either transient or prolonged, through sophisticated programming mechanisms. For instance, viruses that are accountable for causing colds ought to exhibit a level of sophistication that enables them to mislead the body thereby gaining entry into the system. Regrettably, this thesis primarily revolves around economic considerations rather than aligning with factual realities.

The complete physical entity, encompassing not only the brain but also the rest of the body, can be regarded as the utmost intelligent being in organic existence. The human body possesses intricate understanding of the modus operandi of a virus that spreads through nasal inhalation. He permits entry into this system and enables a modification of his own programming. When the body is instructed to cease nasal inhalation, it triggers the restoration of its physiological functions, thereby reinstating the neutralization of the viral infection.

The human body exhibits this response to all viruses and diseases, and the level of trust one has in their body, as well as the thoughts and emotions imparted onto it, will determine the outcome.

In actuality, the physical body possesses a significantly greater understanding of what is beneficial or detrimental for its well-being, compared to the individuality that inhabits it.

Indeed, the latter has a tendency to weaken the physiological state through unfavorable suggestions, particularly facilitated by societal norms that prioritize the individual's character over the intrinsic recuperative abilities of the human body. There is no entity with a more comprehensive understanding of the internal mechanisms of the body than the body itself.

However, there is no better judge of one's physical well-being and mental acuity than the individual themselves, especially if they possess medical knowledge or a sociable disposition. However, the physical form continues to exert control over another remarkable ability that eludes many fields of study - the ability to generate a replica of itself.

The physical entity possesses the capability to regenerate itself - operating strictly on an ethereal or more refined plane. It has the capability to generate a nearly indistinguishable replica of itself. Throughout the course of history, various appellations have been ascribed to this dynamic doppelgänger, encompassing designations such as the ethereal form, the supplementary corporeal vessel, the electrical entity, the astral embodiment, the ethereal conduit, the celestial vehicle, the alternative entity, the energetic manifestation, the psychic manifestation, the bio-plasmic embodiment, and an array of other designations. Regarding my own situation, I typically refer to this corporeal form as the astral body predominantly, alternatively as the second body or as the psycholectrical or electrical body. This act of multiplication fulfills the objective of enduring one's corporeal existence. It exhibits a twofold increase on a nuanced level, rendering it less vulnerable and thereby considerably more resilient.

Furthermore, in conjunction with my numerous instances of disembodiment, I engaged in extensive conversations with diverse individuals concerning the astral form and its corresponding encounters. I was astounded by the multitude of individuals who had encountered such experiences. Indications of this phenomenon consistently exhibit resemblances, and it is my belief that a significant number of individuals have encountered one of the subsequent occurrences at some point in their lives:

Upon waking, one surmises that an earthquake might have occurred.

Upon waking, one recollects having soared in a dream.

Individuals awaken when they perceive a sensation of having been displaced from their original position, or when they suspect that they have been handled by an external force and subsequently returned to their resting place.

Upon awakening, individuals may perceive inexplicable vibrations coursing through their bodies.

Upon awakening, an individual is struck by a profound sense of terror as they discover their incapacitation, leading them to suspect paralysis or the occurrence of a distressing event.

Upon awakening, it is believed that one is experiencing an electrical sensation.

Upon awakening, an individual discovers themselves suspended just below the ceiling.

While you are awake, you perceive it as if someone has intended to disturb or displace you from your bed.

As one emerges into wakefulness or slips into slumber, one abruptly discerns peculiar, synthetically-produced noises.

There are unquestionably additional indications, though the aforementioned ones are the most prevalent.

Certain individuals who possess a penchant for fantastical ideations posit that attaining the second ethereal form embodies the subsequent echelon of lucid dreaming. Furthermore, it is feasible to transition to an alternate corporeal form within the realm of a consciously controlled dream state.

I have personally attempted this technique on numerous occasions and am of the firm belief that it merits a strong recommendation. Furthermore, it has been posited that the second entity possessed the capability to traverse multiple distinct realms.

To establish this concept on your own, it is imperative that you acquire the ability to regulate this secondary entity. To enhance the comprehension of this secondary subject matter, I intend to incorporate several instances that will amplify the intricacies of this procedure:

I retired to bed at a rather late hour with the intention of focusing on inducing an out of body experience. In some manner or another, I must have drifted into slumber, yet soon thereafter I regained consciousness and was seized by a mild sense of fear.

I felt waves running through my whole body, it almost felt as if I were lying in the berth of a ship.

I promptly discerned the presence of my doppelgänger entity just as it was on the verge of departing from my physical being. I maintained a firm grasp, metaphorically speaking, and subsequently commenced the gradual detachment from my corporeal form; however, to my astonishment, I found myself suspended within the very core of my being. There appeared to be an impediment to this process of separation.

I promptly attempted to realign my position by pivoting to both the left and right, yet despite my efforts, I found myself immobilized and incapable of extricating myself from the predicament.

Suddenly I heard footsteps. It appeared as though someone was traversing repeatedly on a weathered hardwood surface. Nevertheless, my residence lacked wooden flooring and was devoid of any creaking noises.

Regrettably, I was unable to visually perceive the individual; however, a certain intuition within me managed to discern their presence to some extent. A male individual awaited me, and the wooden flooring, the abode, and its actuality commenced precisely where my sleeping quarters concluded. The unmistakable sensation of being detached from my physical self and drawn towards him shattered within me. Surprisingly, no further inclination was experienced. After a few further endeavors, my corporeal form gradually stirred, and the two entities once again converged.

In nearly all of my preceding encounters, I consistently prioritized the regulation of the secondary entity. It is a distinct shift in one's ability to gain genuine control, which is often closely tied to the overcoming of fear.

I had been engaged in reading for a period of time, before eventually extinguishing the illumination. As I diligently attended to my second physical form, I anticipated experiencing yet another episode during the course of the evening, exactly as I have done so on preceding nights. In a state of somnolence and diminished focus, I experienced a total absence of consciousness while my physical form lay dormant.

Abruptly, I regained consciousness once more and distinctly sensed the presence of an individual positioned atop my sleeping surface. The surroundings were enveloped in darkness, rendering my vision useless. However, the presence was distinctly palpable to me. I felt a sense of relief, as it seemed that an individual had arrived with the intention of conversing with me or potentially aiding me in transcending my physical form.

Indeed, the aforementioned situation was evident as I observed the act of someone extending their hand beneath my secondary physical form, subsequently raising me from my current position. However, it became evident that there was a disruption occurring as I encountered difficulties in successfully separating from my physical form. I experienced repeated obstructions, impeding a complete detachment from my corporeal existence.

In that instant, recollections of numerous instances flooded my mind wherein such predicaments inevitably arose. Consequently, I vehemently exclaimed my present desire to ascertain the underlying reasons behind my frequent disconnections.

Abruptly, a tremendous shift in my demeanor occurred, and a profound revelation dawned upon me - the presence of an additional facet within my being, whose dissent and dismay became perceptible to me through the lens of extracorporeal encounters. He experienced profound fear and strongly opposed the idea of detachment from his physical being. He vehemently attempted to deter the visitor, who persistently hovered nearby and genuinely sought to offer assistance.

Presently, however, I found myself assuming the role of a 'fearful individual', albeit with the added ability to recollect instances in which I had been unafraid and had initially wholeheartedly supported the release. Notwithstanding the trepidation, I boldly expressed my readiness to fully immerse myself in this encounter, regardless of the potential consequences, even if it were to culminate in my demise. With swift agility, I effortlessly rose from my repose, armed with my corporeal doppelgänger, and prepared myself for imminent departure within the confines of my sleeping quarters. All the complications associated with my release had been resolved.

Controlling Lucid Dreams

Upon the realization that one is in a state of dreaming, it is highly likely that an individual will aspire to exercise control over the dream. It is advisable to carefully orchestrate the sequence of events in order to ensure a positive denouement in the dream. Furthermore, it is imperative to ensure that you devise a viable resolution for each obstacle encountered within the realm of your aspiration. If you have not yet reached a conclusion, it is feasible to shift the focus of your thoughts towards the current predicament you are encountering within the dream.

Prior to embarking upon the manipulation of lucid dreams, it is imperative to grasp the fact that one's experience is confined within the realm of a mere dream. It is imperative to understand that your dreams will remain unknown to others. It is incumbent upon you to comprehend that the responsibility lies with you to determine the course of action regarding the realization of the resolutions made during dreaming.

Once you have comprehended the fact that you are in a state of dreaming, it is imperative to persuade your mind into acknowledging your ability to exercise control over the dream. Instruct your mind to recognize that the situation at hand is merely a figment of imagination, thereby assuring yourself that no adverse consequences shall arise, even if you were to err in your actions or judgments.

When engaging in a state of lucid dreaming, it is advised not to suppress or restrain one's creative urges. Have you ever entertained the idea of something? May I inquire about the approach you employed? Upon the realization that one is experiencing a state of lucid dreaming, it may be constructive to perceive this phenomenon as an imaginative realm.

To exercise command over lucid dreams, simply envision yourself engaged in imaginative reverie. There are no impediments to your ability to accomplish anything within the realm of imagination. Nevertheless, it is imperative that you possess the ability to differentiate between what is feasible and what is unfeasible.

As an illustration, can you recall a moment when you have indulged in the imagination of soaring through the skies or propelling yourself forward at a velocity of 1000 miles per hour? Is that realistic? It is categorically impossible for one to achieve speeds of 1000mph either by flying or running. Nonetheless, you elected to persist with that illusion. Additionally, it is within your power to choose to envision something that is entirely attainable and within the realms of reality. When fantasizing, you can decide to reduce the speed at which you're running to something like 5 or 10 miles per hour. One simply needs to persuade their mind accordingly.

Upon the moment of recognizing one's state of lucidity within a dream, one may exercise the power to deliberate upon altering the unfolding events, thus rendering them incongruous with reality. Alternatively, one can opt for a pragmatic approach and consider attainable endeavors.

Lucid dreams bear a strong resemblance to fantasies. During the state of lucid dreaming, you will possess an awareness of your dream-like state. To exercise dominion over the dream, one must simply instill within oneself the unwavering conviction that one possesses the ability to alter every facet of its unfolding.

As an illustration, one might envision oneself in a state of slumber, imagining being a military personnel stationed in Iraq, whose encampment falls victim to a fierce assault carried out by extremist militants. You currently exhibit concerns regarding potential mortality if appropriate measures are not taken to address your present circumstances. In order to exert influence over the course of events within the dream, one may opt to alter the trajectory of the dream. One could opt to construct a scenario wherein an additional battalion intervenes to provide assistance, eliminating all of the terrorists. By employing this method, you will exert deliberate influence over the dream's outcome and thereby prevent any fatalities.

It is also conceivable that you may be envisioning a scenario wherein your vehicle has malfunctioned in a remote, uninhabited location, leading to your present state of being stranded without any cellular network coverage available in the vicinity. You have made efforts to repair the car, but nonetheless, it is still not starting. Currently, you may be under the impression that the situation cannot deteriorate any further, yet it dawns upon you that the closest town lies hundreds of miles distant. Additionally, the sun is descending below the horizon, and it is common knowledge that this region is abundant with venomous serpents.

What course of action do you intend to pursue at this point? Do you have the means to endure until assistance arrives? It appears highly unlikely that you will survive this predicament. However, it dawns upon you that you had never made arrangements to visit that particular region. Additionally, it is highly unlikely for your vehicle to experience any mechanical failures, given its excellent maintenance record and recent servicing. Hence, it becomes apparent to you that this is nothing more than a mere reverie. You must now persuade your mind to believe that you possess the ability to manipulate the unfolding events within this state of conscious dreaming.

Although the current state of affairs may appear unfavorable, it is essential to acknowledge that you possess the capacity to exert influence over the outcomes within this envisioned reality. You have the option to envision yourself being bitten by a venomous serpent. Alternatively, one may also persuade oneself that they are cognizant of the underlying reasons for the non-functionality of the automobile. Perhaps you inadvertently omitted to reinstall the sparkplug after removing it. Simply ensure that you meticulously reposition the sparkplug, and the vehicle will initiate its operation.

While you remain stranded in that location, you retrieve the sparkplug from its previous placement within the toolbox. Afterward, proceed to unlatch the hood and then carefully place it back in its designated position. Upon activating the vehicle, the engine promptly initiates its operation, at which point your recollection of possessing sufficient fuel to commute to the neighboring town is revived. Now, as you embark upon your journey along the road, a sense of relief washes over you, accompanied by a newfound feeling of contentment, as you become aware that the immediate threat has been averted.

In this reverie, you exercised complete dominion over the unfolding sequence of events, recognizing it to be a state of lucidity. Similarly, you have the ability to exercise control over any lucid dream.

The Manifestation of Desires Through the Veil of Dreams

In the preceding discourse, we have gained knowledge regarding the phenomenon of dream work; it should be acknowledged as a distinctly unique psychological process, one that, to the best of our understanding, bears no resemblance to any other. The concept of the dream has been conveyed a state of confusion which has been provoked within us by its creation. In actuality, the concept of dreamwork merely represents the initial recognition of a cluster of psychological processes from which must be derived the source of hysterical symptoms, the notions of pathological fear, fixation, and delusion. Condensation, and particularly displacement, are constant characteristics in these alternate processes. The emphasis on appearance, however, notably characterizes the collaborative efforts. If this explanation aligns the dream with the development of psychological illness, it becomes crucial to comprehend the fundamental conditions of processes like dream construction. It may come as a surprise to learn that both sleep and illness are not essential conditions. A multitude of occurrences in the everyday lives of healthy individuals, such as forgetfulness, slips in speaking and holding objects, alongside a specific category of errors, can be attributed to a psychological mechanism that bears resemblance to that of dreams and other related phenomena.

Displacement lies at the heart of the issue, and it is the most notable among all the dream manifestations. A comprehensive examination of the subject reveals that the fundamental condition of displacement is solely psychological in nature; it is akin to a motivating factor. We gain insight by examining unavoidable experiences in the analysis of dreams. I had to terminate the connections of my idealistic thoughts during the examination of my dream on paper. I chose not to divulge certain experiences that I encountered, which I believe would be inappropriate to share with unfamiliar individuals, as doing so could potentially harm significant considerations. I added that it would be futile if I were to choose another dream instead of that specific one; in every dream where the meaning is unclear or complex, I should discover dream thoughts that require confidentiality. However, if I were to undertake this analysis independently, without considering the perspectives of others, for whom, it is true, an event such as my dream would not matter, I eventually arrive at ideas that surprise me, ideas that I have not recognized as my own, which not only appear unfamiliar to me, but which are also displeasing, and against which I would like to strongly object, while the sequence of ideas presented in the analysis imposes itself upon me relentlessly. I can only factor in these circumstances by acknowledging that these thoughts are indeed integral to my psychological existence, possessing a certain level of psychological intensity or energy. Nevertheless, due to a specific psychological condition, I was unable to bring the thoughts into my conscious awareness. I designate this particular condition as 'Repression.' Hence, it is inevitable for me to acknowledge certain interconnectedness between the obscurity of the dream content and this state of repression -- this 'incapacity of consciousness'. Based on my analysis, I arrive at the determination that the reason behind the haze is the intention to shield these notions. Therefore, I have reached a conclusion regarding the phenomenon known as dream distortion, which involves the transformation of the dream content, and the use of displacement as a mechanism to conceal the true nature of the dream object.

I shall experiment with this hypothesis within the confines of my personal dream state, and pose the following query to myself: what is the notion that, while seemingly harmless in its altered state, elicits the most vehement resistance in its genuine manifestation? I recall that the complimentary excursion evoked memories of the previous costly outing I had with a family member, with the interpretation of the dream being that I should desire to occasionally undergo such experiences.

The deep affection I harbor towards this individual, for which I should not have to incur costs, and just prior to the dream, I had to make a substantial expenditure for this particular person. In this context, I am unable to escape the notion that I am remorseful for this expenditure. It is only by recognizing this sentiment that there is any justification for my desire to seek an affection that entails no expenditure. I can confidently affirm that

I did not have any reservations whatsoever when it became imperative to allocate that amount. The remorse, the opposing flow, was inconspicuous to me. The reason behind its unconsciousness is a separate issue that would divert us significantly from the answer which, although within my knowledge, pertains elsewhere.

If I were to analyze the dream of another person rather than one of my own, the outcome would remain unchanged; however, the underlying motivations for persuading others would be different. In the idealized vision of a physically sound individual, the lone means by which I can facilitate their embrace of this suppressed concept is through the harmonious consistency of the dream-related cognitions. He retains the freedom to reject this explanation. However, in the case where we are dealing with an individual suffering from a neurosis, such as hysteria, it becomes imperative to acknowledge and address these repressed thoughts due to their association with the symptoms of their illness and the subsequent improvement achieved by replacing the symptoms with the repressed ideas. Kindly escort the individual from whom I obtained the recent recollection regarding the acquisition of three tickets priced at one florin and fifty kreuzers. The analysis reveals that she lacks a favorable opinion of her spouse, expressing remorse for the decision to marry him, and indicating a willingness to exchange him for someone else. Although she maintains her love for her husband and asserts that her emotional well-being remains unaffected by this depreciation (significantly superior, in fact!), all her symptoms point to the same conclusion as this dream. When her suppressed memories resurfaced depicting a certain period when she was conscious of her lack of affection towards her spouse, her symptoms subsided. Consequently, her resistance towards the interpretation of the dream ceased.

Once we establish this understanding of repression, along with the distortion of dreams in relation to repressed psychological content, we are able to provide a comprehensive overview of the key findings that the analysis of dreams offers. We have come to understand that the most comprehensible and profound dreams consist of unattained aspirations, as they project desires that remain unrealized. These desires, presented as realized within the dream, are known to consciousness, derived from the previous waking state, and evoke profound fascination. The examination of obscure and intricate dreams reveals something strikingly similar; the dream scene once again represents a fulfilled desire originating from the dream thoughts, however, the image is unrecognizable and only clarified through the process of analysis. The desire in question is either repressed, beyond conscious awareness, or intricately intertwined with suppressed notions. The formula representing these dreams can be expressed as follows: they are manifestations of repressed desires that are hidden from conscious awareness. It is noteworthy that those who consider the dream as a forecast of what is to come are indeed correct. Despite the fact that the vision depicted in the dream may not align with actual future events, it is reflective of the future outcomes we desire. Folk psychology operates based on its customary manner; it believes what it desires to believe.

Dreams may be categorized into three distinct classes based on their proximity to the attainment of desires. First, we encounter those dreams that manifest an unabashed and undisguised longing. These dreams belong to the category of the infantile variety, which progressively diminish in occurrence among grown individuals. Secondly, dreams that express in concealed form certain suppressed desires; these constitute the majority of our dreams, and they require analysis for their comprehension.

Furthermore, these dreams depict a state of oppression, either present without concealment or with minimal attempt at disguise. These dreams are consistently accompanied by a sensation of apprehension, which ultimately concludes the dream. This sense of apprehension in this context supersedes the displacement of dreams; I perceived the dream analysis as having prevented this in the dream of the second qualm. Demonstrating the current existence of profound apprehension in dreams as a consequence of past longing, which has now become subordinate due to repression, can be established with relative ease.

There are also dreams of a certain nature, characterized by distressing imagery, devoid of any discernible signs of anxiety within the dream. These phenomena cannot be considered as nightmares; nevertheless, they have always been employed to demonstrate the insignificance and the psychological futility of dreams. A careful examination of such an example will reveal that it pertains to our secondary category of dreams--a completely concealed manifestation of suppressed desires. The analysis will illustrate the efficiency of displacement in concealing desires simultaneously.

A young woman had a dream wherein she perceived the lifeless body of her sister's only surviving child, situated in the identical surroundings as she had witnessed a few years prior when she witnessed the death of the first child. She did not appear to experience any discomfort, but instinctively resisted the notion that the scene reflected her own desire. Furthermore, that perspective was not deemed essential. Years ago, it was at the funeral of the child with whom she had previously interacted and conversed with the individual whom she held affection for. If she were to be the second child to pass away, she would undoubtedly encounter this individual once more at her sister's residence. She earnestly desires to encounter him, yet she wrestles with this sentiment. On the day of her reverie, she had procured a ticket for a lecture showcasing the presence of the man she held affection for. The dream represents a form of restlessness commonly experienced prior to embarking on a journey, attending a theatrical performance, or simply anticipating forthcoming pleasures. The yearning is veiled by the transition of the setting to the occasion when any jubilant sentiment was inappropriate, yet where it did once exist. Please be aware that the behavioral response observed in the dream is directed towards the genuine yet repressed dream thoughts, rather than the displaced ones. The setting heralds the highly awaited encounter; there is no cause here for distressing sentiments.

Until now, philosophers have not had reason to engage with a study of psychological repression. It is imperative that we are granted the opportunity to develop a comprehensible understanding regarding the origin of dreams as the initial phases in this unfamiliar domain. The methodology that we have devised, which has been developed not solely through a study of dreams, admittedly possesses a certain level of complexity. However, we have not been able to identify a simpler alternative that would be adequate for our purposes. We assert that within our psychological apparatus, there exist two methodologies for the formation of thoughts. The second approach offers the advantage of allowing its products to become consciously recognized, whereas the first procedure's activity remains unknown to itself and can only attain consciousness through the second approach. At the borderline of these two procedures, where the first merges into the second, a form of censorship is instituted that selectively permits only agreeable content, withholding everything else. The material which is deemed unacceptable by the scrutiny of censorship can be categorized as being in a state of repression, as per our established definition. Under certain circumstances, including the state of sleep, the power dynamics between the two processes are altered to such an extent that repressed elements can no longer be suppressed. In the state of sleep, this may occur due to the inadvertence of the censor; what has been previously suppressed will now succeed in finding its path to consciousness. As the supervision is ever-present, albeit momentarily inattentive, specific modifications must be acknowledged in order to appease its influence. It represents a conscious compromise in this instance - a balancing between the objectives of one procedure and the requirements of the other. Suppression, leniency of the censor, compromise-- these factors serve as the basis for the emergence of numerous psychological processes, much in the same way as they contribute to the formation of dreams. In such compromises, we are able to witness the phenomenon of condensation, displacement, and the acceptance of superficial associations that we have discovered in the dream analysis process.

It is beyond our purview to disregard the malevolent factor that has contributed to shaping our understanding of dream analysis. The overall perception is that the creation of ambiguous dreams seems to occur in a manner similar to one conveying a message or idea that must be agreeable to another individual upon whom they rely for listening. We utilize this image to conceive the idea of the distortion of dreams and the act of censorship, and dared to solidify our impression into a somewhat basic, albeit distinct, psychological theory. Regardless of any forthcoming explanations, it is anticipated that our hypothesis asserting the second procedure's control over consciousness and its ability to exclude the first from consciousness will be affirmed.

After the state of sleep has been overcome, the authority of censorship regains full control and has the capacity to retract what was granted in a moment of vulnerability. The absence of recollection regarding dreams elucidates this phenomenon to a certain extent, as per our empirical observations which continue to affirm this conclusion. Within the course of a dream, or in the process of analyzing one, it is not uncommon for a certain portion of the dream to suddenly be erased from memory. This fragment, which tends to be neglected, consistently encompasses the most effective and readily accessible approach to comprehending the dream. It is likely that this is the reason it becomes forgotten—specifically, within a renewed state of suppression.

Perceiving the content of dreams as the manifestation of a fulfilled longing, and attributing its ambiguity to the alterations imposed by the censor on repressed material, it is no longer arduous to comprehend the purpose of dreams. In stark opposition to those claims positing sleep disruption by dreams, we assert that the dream serves as the protector of sleep. Regarding the aspirations of children, our perspective should be readily embraced.

The state of sleep, regardless of how it is induced, is achieved when the child is sent to sleep or compelled to do so due to exhaustion, with the only assistance being the removal of all stimuli that could activate other objects in the psychological apparatus. The methods that facilitate the maintenance of a considerable separation from external stimuli are well documented; however, what measures can we utilize to alleviate the internal psychological stimuli that hinder sleep? Observe the mother coaxing her child into slumber. The child is persistently requesting; he desires another kiss; he wishes to engage in play for a little longer. His demands are partially fulfilled, while the remainder has been significantly postponed until the subsequent day.

Evidently, these desires and needs that disturb him act as impediments to his ability to sleep. Everyone is familiar with the charming tale of the infamous individual (Baldwin Gröller) who, during the night, would exclaim loudly, "_I desire the rhinoceros_." A truly upstanding individual, instead of exclaiming loudly, would have imagined that they were engaging in playful interaction with the rhinoceros. As the dream that fulfills his desire is held in belief during sleep, it eradicates the desire and renders sleep achievable. It is undeniable that this conviction aligns with the dream imagery, as it is manifested in the psychological manifestation of likelihood; the child lacks the cognitive ability, which they will later acquire, to differentiate hallucinations or fantasies from reality.

The mature individual has acquired this differentiation; he has also acquired an understanding of the futility of desire, and through persistent effort, he is able to delay his aspirations until they can be achieved through some indirect means via a modification in the external environment. Due to this fact, it is uncommon for him to have his desires manifested during moments of sleep in the limited realm of the psyche. It is even plausible that such an occurrence never materializes and that everything that appears to us as a whimsical figment necessitates a significantly more comprehensive elucidation. Thus

It is a delineation of the psychological domain that has been established universally among all rational adults, regardless of any exceptions, which the child was unaware of. A psychological process has been attained which, influenced by life experience, exercises a commanding and restraining influence upon psychological emotions. Through its connection to consciousness and its inherent spontaneity, it possesses the utmost capacity for psychological power. A portion of the infantile emotions has been withheld from this procedure as they are deemed irrelevant to life, and all the thoughts that arise from these emotions are found in a state of repression.

While the process in which we recognize our normal ego reposes upon the desire for sleep, it appears compelled by the psychophysiological conditions of sleep to relinquish some of the energy with which it was accustomed during the day to suppress what was repressed. This negligence is relatively benign; although the child's emotions may be stirred to some extent, they encounter difficulty in attaining consciousness and their movement is subsequently impeded due to the state of sleep. The danger of their disturbing sleep must, however, be avoided. Furthermore, it is important to acknowledge that even during deep sleep, a certain amount of conscious attention is exerted as a safeguard against external stimuli that could potentially make awakening appear more prudent than the continuation of sleep. Otherwise, we would be unable to account for the phenomenon of our incessant arousal through stimuli of a specific nature. As the renowned physiologist Burdach noted, the mother is aroused from her slumber by the faint cries of her child, the miller by the halt of his mill, and the majority of individuals by the tender invocation of their names. This heightened awareness, therefore, utilizes the internal stimuli that emerge from suppressed desires, and amalgamates them into the dream, which, as a compromise, satisfies both mechanisms simultaneously. The dream serves as a mechanism of psychological release for desires that are either suppressed or brought about through the assistance of repression, as it presents them as achieved or fulfilled. The other procedure is equally satisfactory, as it guarantees the uninterrupted continuation of sleep. Our self here willingly assumes a childlike demeanor; it renders the imaginary scenes convincing, saying, so to speak, 'Yes, that's right, but let me sleep.' The contempt that we bear the dream upon awakening, and that rests upon the absurdity and apparent illogicality of the dream, is likely nothing more than the reasoning of our sleeping self on the emotions associated with what was repressed; with even greater justification, it should be based on the inadequacy of this disturber of our sleep. During periods of slumber, there are occasional instances in which we become cognizant of a sense of disdain. The content of our dreams surpasses the level of censorship we deem appropriate, prompting us to conclude, "It is merely a fabrication of the mind," and we continue to rest.

There is no objection to this perspective if there are limitations for the subconscious state in which its purpose is to ensure the continuity of sleep is no longer sustained, as seen in dreams of imminent fear. It has been altered here for a different purpose - to effectively interrupt the sleep at the appropriate moment. It functions as a diligent night-watchman, who first fulfills his obligation to suppress disruptions so as not to disturb the citizen, but equally fulfills his obligation quite appropriately when he awakens the street should the causes of the trouble appear to him as serious and himself unable to manage them alone.

This phenomenon of dreams becomes particularly pronounced when there emerges some stimulus for the sensory perception. It is widely acknowledged in scientific research that the stimulation of the senses during sleep influences dreams, and this relationship has been successfully validated through empirical experimentation. Consequently, this finding stands as a reliable yet frequently exaggerated outcome of medical investigations pertaining to dreams. Thus far, a perplexing enigma has been associated with this revelation. The sensory stimulation exerted by the investigator on the sleeper is not adequately acknowledged in the dream, but rather intertwined with various indefinite interpretations, the determination of which seems to be left to psychological volition. There is, naturally, no existence of psychic free will. The sleeper can respond to an external sensory stimulus in various manners. Either he awakens or he attains sleep. In the latter scenario, he can utilize the dream to disregard the external stimulus, and this can be done in multiple manners. For example, he can prevent the stimulus from affecting him by envisioning a situation that he finds completely unbearable. This was the method employed by an individual who was afflicted with a distressing perineal abscess. He had a dream in which he found himself on horseback, employing the poultice that was intended to alleviate his discomfort as a saddle, thus escaping the source of the problem. Alternatively, and as is more commonly observed, the external stimulus undergoes a new interpretation, prompting the individual to associate it with a suppressed desire seeking fulfillment. This process usurps its objective reality, treating it as an integral component of the psychological realm. Therefore, an individual dreamed that they had authored a comedic piece that embodied a distinct theme; it was being presented on stage; the initial act concluded amidst enthusiastic applause; there was significant clapping. At this moment, the visionary must have successfully extended his slumber despite the disturbance, for upon awakening, he no longer perceived the auditory disturbance. He accurately inferred that someone must have been engaging in the act of beating a carpet or bed. The dreams that arise with a significant sound prior to awakening have all endeavored to obscure the stimuli of awakening through alternative explanations, thereby prolonging sleep momentarily.

Any individual who has fully embraced this concept of "censorship" as the primary impetus behind the manipulation of dreams will not be taken aback to discover, through the process of dream interpretation, that the majority of adults' dreams can be attributed, upon analysis, to erotic longings. This assertion is not derived from dreams that clearly pertain to sexual themes, which are widely recognized by all dreamers based on their personal experiences, and are typically referred to as "sexual dreams." These dreams possess a certain level of mystique due to the selection of individuals who become the subjects of sexual desire, the removal of all inhibitions that restrain the dreamer's sexual needs in their waking state, and the numerous peculiar reminders of details associated with what are commonly referred to as perversions. However, analysis reveals that in many other dreams where no explicit erotic content is apparent in the manifest content, interpretation shows them to be, in fact, manifestations of sexual desires. Conversely, much of the thinking that occurs during wakefulness, consisting of thoughts that are surplus from the day, finds representation in dreams through the aid of repressed erotic desires.

In order to elucidate this statement, which is not a mere hypothetical postulate, it must be borne in mind that no other category of instincts has necessitated such extensive suppression at the behest of civilization as the sexual instincts, while their mastery through the highest psychological processes is relinquished by most individuals at the earliest opportunity. Given our acquired knowledge of infantile sexuality, which is often expressed in ambiguous and easily overlooked ways, it is justifiable to assert that almost every civilized individual has retained, at some point or another, the infantile form of sexual life. Consequently, we understand that repressed infantile sexual desires provide the most prevalent and influential motivations for the creation of dreams.

If the dream, which represents a specific erotic longing, manages to present its true content in an innocent and non-sexual manner, it can only be achieved in one particular manner. The depiction of these sexual presentations cannot be displayed as is, but must be substituted with allusions, suggestions, and similar indirect methods. Unlike other instances of indirect representation, the ones used in dreams must be devoid of direct comprehension. The means of presentation that satisfy these requirements are commonly referred to as "symbols." There has been a particular focus on these symbols, as it has been observed that individuals who speak the same language tend to use similar symbols in their dreams. In fact, in certain cases, there is a greater shared understanding through symbols than through spoken language. As the individuals who envision these symbols are not inherently aware of their meaning, it remains an enigma to decipher their relationship with the concepts they represent and signify. The fact itself is indisputable and becomes significant for the technique of interpreting dreams, as through an understanding of this symbolism, it is possible to comprehend the meaning of the elements or components of a dream, occasionally even the entire dream itself, without needing to inquire about the dreamer's personal thoughts. Therefore, we draw close to the prevailing concept of interpreting dreams whilst simultaneously reclaiming the methods of ancient civilizations, wherein the interpretation of dreams was synonymous with elucidation through symbolism.

Despite the abstract nature of studying dream symbolism, we currently have a collection of general statements and specific observations that are highly conclusive. Symbols that consistently retain the same meaning include Emperor and Empress (King and Queen), which invariably represent the parents. Similarly, the symbol of a room, a woman[2], and so forth, also holds a consistent connotation. The genders are represented by numerous symbols, some of which may initially be difficult to understand if not for the hints to their meaning being frequently obtained through alternative channels.

Symbols of universal circulation can be observed in the dreams of all individuals, regardless of their linguistic or cultural background. Conversely, there are symbols that hold a highly specific personal significance, which are constructed by an individual based on their own unique experiences. In the first category, individuals can be distinguished based on the immediate recognition of their claims through the substitution of sexual terms in everyday language (such as those pertaining to agriculture, like reproduction and seed). In contrast, the sexual references made by those in the second category seem to originate from the earliest times and delve into the most elusive depths of our image construction. The potency of constructing symbols in both these distinctive manifestations of symbols has not waned. Recently discovered innovations, such as the airship, have swiftly become universally embraced as symbolic representations of sexuality.

It would be erroneous to assume that possessing a deeper understanding of dream symbolism, commonly known as the "Language of Dreams," would render us independent of questioning the dreamer regarding their impressions about the dream. Moreover, such knowledge would not restore to us the complete methodology employed by ancient dream interpreters. In addition to individual symbols and variations in the use of what is generally accepted, one can never ascertain whether an element in the dream is to be understood symbolically or in its literal sense; the entire content of the dream is certainly not to be interpreted symbolically. The comprehension of dream symbols will merely assist us in interpreting certain aspects of the dream content, and does not render the application of the technical guidelines previously provided as redundant in any way. However, it would be immensely beneficial in the realm of dream interpretation if the dreamer's impressions were either withheld or proved to be inadequate.

Dream symbolism is also essential in comprehending both the "typical" dreams and the recurring dreams. It transcends the realm of dreams, extending its significance to legends, myths, sagas, humor, and folklore. It necessitates our pursuit of the inherent significance of the dream in these productions. However, it is essential to acknowledge that symbolism is not a direct outcome of the dream work, but rather a distinct characteristic likely stemming from our unconscious cognition. This aspect provides the raw material for condensation, displacement, and dramatization within the dream work.

The "Wake Back To Bed Technique"

The Wake Back To Bed Technique can be considered as the most accessible approach for novices, presenting the highest probability of achieving positive outcomes. For this reason, we will commence by providing a detailed overview of this method. As indicated by its name, the fundamental concept underlying this technique is to rouse oneself in the morning for a specified interval, thereafter resuming sleep with the intention of inducing a state of lucid dreaming. Given that this methodology necessitates rousing oneself and subsequently returning to slumber, it is advisable to engage in its practice during weekends or holidays, when it is unlikely to encroach upon one's customary obligations, such as professional or educational engagements.

In order to employ the Wake Back To Bed Technique, we configure an alarm to activate in the morning, one hour prior to our usual awakening time. Subsequently, we proceed to retire for the evening in our usual manner, as the majority of the efficacy of this strategy will manifest early in the morning. One may find it beneficial, though, to engage in the practice of silently reciting affirmative statements to oneself before drifting off to sleep, such as "Tonight, I shall experience a lucid dream" or "I will become aware that I am dreaming."

Upon awakening in the morning, it is crucial to refrain from opening your eyes or making any movements. The occurrence of any bodily movements will impede the recollection of dreams and initiate the process of awakening your physical body, leading to a greater distance from the state of sleep.

While remaining in a supine position, reflect upon your recent period of dormancy and inquire within, "Upon what subject matter did my slumber bestow?" Dedicate a couple of fleeting moments to diligently recollect as many intricacies of your dream as can be summoned to consciousness. Make an effort to recollect the overarching context of the dream, alongside precise particulars such as visual elements, auditory cues, olfactory sensations, and so forth.

Once you have recollected the dream for a brief period, proceed to open your eyes and promptly rise from your bed. This measure is crucial in order to prevent recurrences of drowsiness. It is recommended that you proceed with transferring as much pertinent information that you have recollected into your designated dream journal at this juncture. Exercise heightened awareness towards 'dream signs' – these are elements within the dream that appear incongruous or illogical, which could have potentially alerted one to the realization of being in a dream state; examples include opening a door leading to outer space, conversing with animals, or encountering other nonsensical phenomena. When you choose to resume sleeping at a later time, it is imperative that you exercise heightened vigilance in order to identify and take note of these indicators within your dreams. Furthermore, it is worth noting that dream signs frequently manifest consistently in dreams over the course of multiple nights or weeks. Recognizing and discerning these recurring patterns can also facilitate the attainment of lucidity within a dream.

There exist numerous indications that may serve as clues to the recognition of being in a dream. However, during moments of non-lucidity, it is often effortless to unquestioningly embrace the elements presented within the dream as veracious. This encompasses instances where objects diverge in size from their real-world counterparts, situations involving the presence of acquaintances or family members from different countries, and even the experience of heightened emotions such as significantly increased sadness or anger, surpassing one's ordinary waking-life encounters.

After you have finished documenting all the specific details to the best of your recollection, it will be necessary for you to remain awake for one hour before resuming your bedtime routine. During this period, we will endeavor to inspire ourselves and cultivate a constructive mindset with the aim of experiencing a lucid dream prior to retiring for the night. This brief period spanning from waking up to going back to bed can effectively enhance wakefulness and heighten mental acuity, thereby increasing the likelihood of sustaining a state of lucidity.

To cultivate motivation, one may engage in the act of witnessing a profoundly inspiring audiovisual testimony, such as a cinematic vignette or musical composition that stirs the soul and instills a sense of fervor. For instance, should one desire to venture to the lunar surface within the realm of their lucid dreaming, they could partake in the observation of audiovisual documentation pertaining to the historic moon landing or various space shuttle expeditions. Make a conscious effort to immerse yourself in the depicted scenario while observing it.

After the conclusion of your designated wakefulness period, you may proceed to the bed and make necessary arrangements to facilitate your return to slumber. Please ensure that you are at ease and in a state of relaxation. A technique that can assist in achieving a state of relaxation is the systematic tensing and releasing of each muscle group in the body, starting from the feet and progressively moving towards the head. After closing your eyes and striving to return to sleep, it may be beneficial to envision yourself revisiting the dream you experienced earlier in the morning and endeavor to mentally place yourself within it. Engage in a thorough rehearsal of the complete dream sequence once more, with the purpose of envisioning yourself attaining lucidity and assuming command over the dream. Reiterate within your mind as you drift back into slumber, "I intend to acknowledge that I am in a state of dreaming."

You may need to conduct trial and error with different wake-up times as you implement this technique. If the time chosen is too early, it is probable that one might experience excessive drowsiness, thereby hindering the ability to maintain sufficient levels of awareness required for the occurrence of a lucid dream. If you rise belatedly, you may encounter challenges when attempting to return to slumber.

PROS:

- Simple

- It can prove to be highly dependable, particularly when complemented with other methodologies.

CONS:

- One must awaken at a different hour, leading to potential disturbance of the sleep cycle.

- It is impractical for instances where one has fixed work or school schedules that require them to wake up at specific times.

www.ingramcontent.com/pod-product-compliance
Lightning Source LLC
Chambersburg PA
CBHW050243120526
44590CB00016B/2193